cape town
flavours and traditions

JACANA

Lourensford Wine Estate, Somerset West   Previous page: V&A Waterfront

Cape of Good Hope Nature Reserve

Introduction

Spices that we add to our food every day without thinking, such as pepper, cinnamon, cloves and nutmeg, were such a valuable commodity in the 15th-century that they inspired fearless mariners to cross vast oceans in less than adequate vessels in search of new routes to the spice-rich Orient. And so the world map began to change and grow due to adventurous Portuguese mariners whose exploration reached down Africa's western coastline. And, in 1486, they managed successfully to round the southernmost tip of Africa. Suddenly the Cape featured on all of their maps.

For a brief period the Cape became known as the Cape of Storms due to the rough seas caused by gale-force winds. The storms persisted, but were soon eclipsed by the fascination people developed about the growing legend of the Cape and all it had to offer. It was subsequently dubbed the Cape of Good Hope for it became symbolic of long-awaited success in the quest for a sea route connecting Europe to the East.

On one of the voyages past this tip of Africa, a Dutch ship dropped anchor at the Cape to collect passengers who had been stranded there for a few months. On board this ship was a doctor, Jan van Riebeeck, who noticed the abundance of fresh water flowing down from Table Mountain, as well as the fertile soil and rich marine life. Knowing how many sailors died due to scurvy, he began to dream of a settlement producing fresh produce and supplying fresh water to the passing ships. This dream became reality on his return voyage to the Cape when, on 6 April 1652, three Dutch ships approached the magnificent sight of unspoilt Table Mountain and he set foot on dry land to begin work.

Soon the Cape became known as The Tavern of the Seas as the sight of Table Mountain became the invitation to all travelling foodies to enjoy the treasures of the Cape table. And, today, Cape cuisine and hospitality still delight many visitors to our breathtakingly beautiful city.

So, welcome! We invite you to explore our unique tapestry of flavours and hope you will stop awhile and enjoy the stories and food at our Cape table.

The Cape Table

Culinary traditions at the Cape should be seen as a melting pot of influences from the various nationalities that called this home. We inherited stories, traditions and tried-and-tested family recipes from these adventurous explorers. A fusion of Dutch, English, French, German, indigenous tribes and Malay slaves formed the basis of our local culinary traditions, many of which are still practised today.

Table Mountain from Bloubergstrand 19

The Strandlopers

An indigenous tribe was found at the Cape by the early Dutch settlers who aptly dubbed them *Strandlopers* (beach strollers, nomads). These people lived in harmony with nature, depending on their surroundings for their food supply.

They were quintessential hunter-gatherers whose intimate knowledge of and close relationship with nature afforded them a steady supply of edible indigenous plant material, some of it medicinal. In addition, their primitive but effective hunting and fishing skills kept them supplied with fresh protein.

The Dutch

It was the Dutch who gave birth to food production at the Cape on their arrival in 1652. At first the settlers followed the example of the *Strandlopers* and turned to nature for their culinary needs. Plants like wild mustard and wild sorrel were harvested. But never content with letting local grass grow under their feet, within 14 days of landing, they laid out a vegetable garden and soon a steady supply of seeds for cultivation was arriving from abroad.

This led to a vast variety of greens in the Cape in the late 1600s and here the practice of serving an array of vegetables with every meal was established. The Dutch served boiled vegetables: their favourites were gem squash and potatoes with a blob of butter and grated nutmeg. A tradition that persists to this day.

Initially four cooks from the Dutch ships were responsible for all of the cooking. They stuck to what was familiar to them and very little change in the style of the meals took place. But farms were granted to families in 1657 and the women began preparing meals for their families to enjoy – each developing their own cooking style – and so the unique character of Cape cuisine began to unfold.

The wife of the head gardener at the Company's Garden (where food was produced for passing ships) was Annetjie Boom*. She opened the first inn at the Cape where, other than providing sailors with a bed, she had a platform to experiment with ingredients and create new dishes to serve her guests.

*Serendipitously 'boom' is the Afrikaans word for tree.

In 1665 a market was started where farmers could sell their produce at fixed prices as determined by the governor. Menus were simple but the list of ingredients was growing. So much so that by the end of the 17th-century the new governor at the Cape, Simon van der Stel, wrote to the Dutch government of the time that the settlers were satisfied with life at the Cape and really needed nothing more. The growing availability and variety of fresh produce led to the development of a unique cookery style.

In the Netherlands at the time, meat and fish dishes were prepared using herbs and spices and that custom continued at the Cape. Many Dutch recipes have been etched into our story and dishes such as *frikkadels* (meatballs) are still prepared to this day, while remaining virtually unknown in the Netherlands. Pies and fruit tarts were very popular – as were pancakes – all of which are still favourites in the Cape.

Visitors to the late 17th-century Cape reported that the food here was better than back home, and the Cape's reputation as one of the food capitals of the world began to grow.

The French

The status quo at the Cape shifted with the arrival of the French Huguenots who took farming practices further inland. They arrived before the era of famous French chefs, so the style of cuisine they brought with them could best be described as simple. Beautiful farms were established in Franschhoek, which means French corner, so named for the concentration of Huguenots who settled there. Although their cooking style lacked the sophistication that we associate with classic French cuisine today, it definitely added a new dimension to Cape cookery.

Where the Dutch used a lot of fat, the French drained all excess fat and delicately flavoured their dishes with herbs. Not many spices were used so flavours were subtler.

Furthermore, the French introduced the tradition of serving several courses at one meal. Up until then, the Dutch would place the entire meal on the table at once. Now soup was served first followed by the main course, and then dessert which was usually fresh fruit. This change led to what we currently know as menu courses.

Cuts of animals that were not previously used were prepared by the French and offal – especially tripe and trotters – became a regular delicacy.

The Huguenots were experienced farmers who contributed greatly to the improvement of viticulture and fruit farming. They also created innovative dishes from the local fruit. For example, they left a legacy with *boerejongens* and *boeremeisies* which are raisins and apricots preserved in brandy. Using other fruits, they made delicious confitures (jams) that are still enjoyed at the Cape and are known as *konfyt* in Afrikaans.

Although they influenced Cape cuisine, it was never an overpowering influence as there were not many French at the Cape at any time. And as their farms were in and amongst those of the Dutch, the cultural identities soon became blurred. As its name implies, Franschhoek became the Gallic epicentre of the Cape and still today remains a name closely associated with gastronomic excellence.

The Malay Slaves

But it was the arrival of the first Malay slaves in 1657 that brought about the biggest change to local cuisine. This group of people was called Malay because of a communal language that they spoke in order to understand one another. They hailed from different parts of the world – not, as is commonly assumed, from Malaysia – and had to find a way to communicate.

At the time of their arrival, the Dutch controlled Indonesia, and the headquarters for the Dutch East India Company – commonly referred to as the VOC (*Vereenigde Oost-Indische Compagnie*) – was on the island of Java, where the first slaves came from. The men were experienced carpenters, tailors, musicians, coachmen, fishermen and plasterers, and most of the ornate gables towering above the entrances to traditional Cape Dutch homesteads were skilfully done by them freehand.

The women were lace makers and experienced cooks. With them came flavours from the East which were introduced to Cape kitchens in the form of inventive dishes from their countries of origin using spices that they brought with them. Curries were introduced. These were adapted by almost totally replacing chillies and green ginger – important elements of Oriental curries – with ingredients like orange leaves, dried apricots and chutney. Today one can still distinguish between traditional Oriental curries and what we call Malay curries – the latter being aromatic with a hint of sweetness, combining subtle spices and dried fruit rather than packing the heat that characterises their Oriental counterparts. The art of combining a variety of spices in one dish was introduced by the Malays and is still practised.

The Malay cooks introduced meaty curries which went down very well with the settlers. Soon dishes such as *bobotie* (a curried minced meat dish with raisins and other fruit and topped with a baked savoury custard), *sosaties* (kebabs) and *bredie* (stew) became favourites in Cape homes. Traditionally *bobotie* is served with yellow rice.

yellow rice

Serves 4

METHOD

- Bring the water and salt to the boil. Add the rice and cook it in the water with the turmeric until soft – about 15 minutes. Drain and rinse under cold running water.
- Place the yellow rice in a colander over a saucepan of boiling water. Add the cinnamon quills and raisins. Steam until the rice is fluffy and the raisins are puffed. Make sure the water in the saucepan does not boil dry.
- Add the honey and butter and mix them into the rice using a fork.

INGREDIENTS

1 litre water
1 tsp salt
1 cup rice
2 tsp turmeric
2 quills of cinnamon
½ cup raisins
30 ml honey
2 tbsp butter

Traditionally bobotie is served with yellow rice

Tip: If this is served as an accompaniment to bobotie (see the recipe on page 113) which already contains raisins, replace the raisins in this recipe with half a cup of lightly toasted flaked almonds. Add the almonds at the last minute with the honey and butter.

Sambals were introduced and various pickles and fruit chutneys were created too.

The wives of expert Malay fishermen transformed their husbands' catch into innovative dishes such as pickled fish and fish grilled over coals. *Bokkoms* (kippered Cape herring) were a substitute for the people living too far north to enjoy the abundant fresh fish at the Cape.

So great was the influence of the Malay people on Cape cuisine that today *bobotie* served with yellow rice and raisins, as well as *malva* pudding, are considered national dishes.

The Germans

Many young German sailors began to arrive at the Cape with the first ships, soon followed by teachers and artisans. Most of them arrived as bachelors who later married local girls, so diluting their authentic German culinary traditions. However, they left an indelible mark on Cape cuisine in the form of a wide variety of sausages, especially *boerewors* (literally translated as farmers' sausage) which can be found in supermarkets and on every butcher's counter.

Today there is a large German population in the Cape, especially in Somerset West, with a flourishing German language school at the foot of Lion's Head.

Watsonias on the Helderberg mountain range

The English

By the time the 1820 Settlers arrived from Britain, the Cape had an established cookery tradition. However, to this day hotels in and around Cape Town serve high tea with scones, jam and cream, as well as cucumber sandwiches, apple pie and trifle, to name a few, indicating that the English too left a mark on our food map.

Another British tradition, fish and chips, is a firm favourite at the Cape.

Contemporary Influences

The passion for food and ingredients and experimentation has continued and people who visit this part of the world still enjoy lingering beside a traditional and contemporary Cape table.

Today you can pick and choose from a plethora of flavours and influences from places like Japan, Thailand, India, France, Greece, Portugal, China, Vietnam, Turkey, Lebanon and more – all of which have influenced our journey to gourmet pleasure in some form or another.

Table Mountain

The sight of Table Mountain towering above Table Bay, like a sentinel keeping watch over this unspoilt terrain, must have been as spectacular to those who sailed in and out of Table Bay in the early days as it is today. It is no surprise that this prominent landmark was voted one of the New 7 Wonders of the World. From a geological point of view, this flat-topped mountain dates back approximately 260 million years, predating the Andes, Rockies, Himalayas and Alps.

The present-day city of Cape Town has been developed around Table Mountain – specifically around the principal part of the range that extends all the way from Table Bay to Cape Point, the south-western tip of Africa, where the cold Benguela current hugs its coast on the western side and the warmer Agulhas current on the eastern side. All this has given our city and its surrounds a unique climate that contributes to the cultivation of vines, as well as a unique abundance of sea life. Today there are many wine estates in the foothills of Table Mountain, but most of the areas where farming was once practised have surrendered to suburban sprawl.

Aerial view of Cape Town

This extraordinary slice of topography has been declared a national park as well as a World Heritage Site. It supports the richest diversity of flora in the world and contains the highest concentration of threatened species of any other similar-sized area on this planet.

Table Mountain, the gateway to the range, has approximately 2 200 plant species that form a part of the *fynbos* (fine bush) biome.

These are confined to the level plateau of about three kilometres from side to side – some of them endemic to that part of the mountain. This is more than exists in the entire United Kingdom. *Fynbos* plants have hardy stems and fine leaves that limit moisture loss in the prevailing winds. These plants depend on natural wild fires that occur seasonally for seed dispersal and new growth.

Twelve Apostles, Table Mountain

Because of the topography, the summit height of 1 086 metres and summer's prevailing south-easterly wind blowing moisture from the warmer Indian Ocean towards the back of the eastern slopes of Table Mountain, what Capetonians refer to as a tablecloth can often be seen slowly creeping over the mountain towards Table Bay. This cloud cover causes sufficient condensation and precipitation to ensure that water trickles and flows down the mountain for most of the year. Very occasionally it will snow on Table Mountain.

Hiking, rock climbing, caving, paragliding and birding are a few of the activities that are enjoyed on these slopes. The cableway transports (literally and figuratively) about 800 000 visitors to the top of the table each year where they encounter panoramic views over Table Bay and Robben Island, as well as southwards to where Cape Point disappears into the sea mist en route to Antarctica...

Wine

Today's wine industry contributes to Cape Town's appeal as one of the top tourist destinations in the world. The story begins in 1655 with Jan van Riebeeck planting the first vines in the Cape, and with the first wine produced locally four years later.

In the early days, because coffee and tea were unknown to the settlers, Van Riebeeck wrote in his journal that wine, brandy and beer were served with meals – yes, even at breakfast! Today there is such an entrenched culture of coffee and tea in Cape Town, including our locally produced rooibos tea, that it seems impossible ever to have had breakfast at the Cape without a cup of tea or coffee.

Van Riebeeck was so excited about the latent potential for wine production that he encouraged the local farmers to plant vines on a larger scale, starting in areas today known as Wynberg and Bishopscourt. But farmers were reluctant to embark on this venture mainly due to their limited knowledge of viticulture. This changed, however, when Simon van der Stel was appointed governor in 1679. Not only was his enthusiasm infectious, but it was grounded in a vast knowledge of viticulture and viniculture which ultimately led to better quality wines. He planted 100 000 vines in the Constantia valley and, in 1685, was granted the farm Groot Constantia on the eastern slopes of Table Mountain which is still operational today. He imported oak trees, hoping to produce wood for local barrel manufacturing, but our warmer climate caused the trees to grow faster than in Europe and the wood was too porous to use. Today oak trees dating back to that time can be seen all over the Cape, some of them considered national monuments and protected by law.

Despite Van der Stel's contribution, the Dutch came with a limited history of wine making. So with the arrival of the Huguenots in 1688 dawned a new era in wine culture and

skills that left a definite impact on our wine industry and, consequently, on life in the Cape. The Huguenots were religious refugees who arrived here with very little money and had to make do with the bare minimum. As a result, established wine-making techniques had to be adapted to local conditions.

Various cultivars were brought to the Cape by the passing Dutch ships. These were mainly from France, Spain and Persia (Iran today) and were planted from cuttings. By the early 1800s the main grape variety by far was Semillon, a variety many are inclined to think of as a recent innovation.

Due to a scarcity of labour, everyone pitched in to make the harvest experience positive and to ensure a smooth process. It was not general practice at the Cape to mature wines as most of the farmers lacked the expertise and were still grappling with local conditions so unlike those in Europe.

Furthermore, only the wealthy farmers had the means to purchase enough vats for maturation purposes. Today our international award-winning wines are matured successfully and, although some oak is imported from America, the bulk is imported from France.

During the 18th and 19th centuries, the only great wines being produced in the southern hemisphere were the sweet wines produced at Van der Stel's farm, Groot Constantia. In fact, during this time, these dessert wines were the most prized in the world, beguiling kings and emperors alike.

Legend has it that Napoleon, while in exile on St Helena Island between 1815 and 1821, asked for a glass of Constantia wine on the evening of his death. The wine was also celebrated by writers and poets, and in *Sense and Sensibility*, Mrs Jennings recommends a glass of Constantia wine for its 'healing powers on a disappointed heart'.

In the early 20th-century, a young Cape Town professor of French descent, who had obtained a PhD in chemistry in Germany, was sent on a mission overseas as the Cape government wanted to expand the range of grape cultivars that was being produced. He returned with 177 varietals which formed the basis of an experiment on a farm outside Stellenbosch. Soon thereafter he was appointed as the first Professor of Viticulture at the University of Stellenbosch, the first of many stops on his journey through the wine industry in the Cape where he left an indelible footprint in the form of Pinotage, South Africa's only signature cultivar.

This man, Professor Abraham Izak Perold, had a vast knowledge of the grape varieties of the world. And so, when he selected the two varieties that he hybridised to produce Pinotage, everyone thought it strange. Why would one cross Pinot Noir, the prince of French red grapes, with Hermitage (also known as Cinsaut) which, other than doing well locally, was a much humbler variety? He left no clues. Four humble little seedlings were produced, and Perold planted these in his home garden where he could keep a keen eye on them and chart their progress.

But the four seedlings in time were forgotten and Perold moved house when he left the university to work elsewhere in the industry. The garden became overgrown and the seedlings buried somewhere in the undergrowth. One morning, when the university had sent a team of workers out to clear the garden, another young lecturer, who had known about Perold's experiment, passed by on his bicycle. He

stopped and saved the seedlings, and the rest is history.

The first Pinotage wine was created in 1941. Today various estates produce this unique wine, and Pinotage, thanks to Perold, is enjoyed all around the world. It took a long time for Pinotage to become a world-renowned wine, but it did, winning various awards both locally and internationally.

Although many wine farms have been handed down from generation to generation, foreign investment has recently seen overseas buyers add funding and expertise to further the local industry's insatiable quest for world-class quality and international recognition.

Wine tours are presented by most estates, and visitors to the Cape have a choice between farms with old-world charm and those with cutting-edge technology – and often these qualities exist side by side.

Brandy

The word brandy comes from the Dutch word *brandewijn,* which literally means burnt or distilled wine. The Dutch, who at the time were the foremost seafaring nation in Western Europe, imported vast quantities of brandy, mainly from Cognac, for the enjoyment of their sailors during their voyages.

By the late 16th-century, wine-making techniques had not yet evolved to the point where natural wine could be prevented from spoiling after just a few months, and so wine would never survive from one vintage to the next. Brandy, on the other hand, was more resilient, and with the increasing global influence of the Dutch well into the 17th-century, their term *brandewijn* soon gained worldwide acclaim.

Twenty years after their arrival at the Cape, brandy was first distilled by one of the chefs from a passing Dutch ship. It was then, as it is now, made by distilling wine into a pure spirit. Today in South Africa, by law, this spirit must then be matured in small French oak barrels for at least three years before it is blended to each brandy master's special recipe. The reason for the small barrels is that they enhance the intensity of the flavours imparted by the wood.

South Africa has a brandy-producing history that spans three-and-a-half centuries, and this country is the fifth-largest producer of brandy in the world today. Although the majority is consumed locally, the demand for South African brandy is growing worldwide as more and more people are exposed to it. South African brandies have fared extremely well in international competitions and have had a consistent run of victories in recent years.

The grapes for making brandy are picked earlier than the grapes used for table wines, when they have higher acidity levels and

lower sugar levels. Although sulphur dioxide is commonly used in the preservation of normal wines, no preservatives are used in the production of base wine for brandy production. The higher acid content in the grapes acts as a natural preservative. The base wine is furthermore distilled almost immediately and stored at low temperatures with as little exposure to oxygen as possible. This process is aided by using yeast sediment that further prevents oxygen from reacting with flavour compounds in the wine.

Any cultivars can be used for brandy production but Chenin Blanc and Colombar are currently responsible for 90 percent of base wine production. Each grape variety adds a different character and taste profile that will influence the end product. One of the main cultivation areas for brandy grapes is Worcester, which is about a 90-minute drive from the heart of Cape Town.

Brandy is South Africa's top-selling spirit drink with average annual sales of more than 45 million litres. Its popularity seems to be due to its versatility, as it can be enjoyed neat, on ice, with various non-alcoholic mixers or in cocktails. It is also widely used in our local cuisine, both modern and traditional, in dishes such as brandy tart, *Kaapsche Jongens* (brandied *Hanepoot* grapes), *Boerejongens* (brandied raisins) and *Boeremeisies* (brandied apricots).

Grain

One of the main wheat-based culinary traditions that was developed at the Cape – and indeed throughout South Africa – is the rusk: a biscotti-like creation baked in the form of a loaf of bread, and then cut or broken into smaller, more manageable pieces that are dried in an oven for a few hours and enjoyed by dunking into coffee and tea.

The early ancestors of present-day rusks, also called *skeepsbroot* (ship's bread) or *tweebacken* (twice baked) were made from wheat flour and were the staple food on the ships. Van Riebeeck took the task of providing nourishment to the passing ships very seriously and, wanting to provide a local source of rusks and other wheat-based products, he saw to it that the first wheat was sown in the Company's Garden in July 1652.

But destructive storms, strong winds, wild animals and plant lice plagued this crop to such an extent that a quarter of the expected crop was harvested the following January. Still, they continued their attempts to grow wheat in Table Bay successfully. The process was slow as storms at the Cape continued their devastating patterns.

The cultivation of grain became such an issue that Van Riebeeck began to enforce wheat cultivation. Despite experimenting with various locations, it took close to 40 years before enough wheat was produced near

Stellenbosch to satisfy both local demand, as well as exports to Batavia.

Today our main wheat production area, which we refer to as the Swartland – literally meaning black land or black earth, so called because of the blackish colour of the local vegetation – is the area around Malmesbury, Moorreesburg and Porterville. After the initial lack of success, this area was established around 1720 and has become the mainstay of the country's wheat production, which today is used mainly for flour.

Other grains that are successfully produced in the Cape are crops like canola, oats, lupins and rye. Vast splashes of yellow colour the contours of the mountainous farming area around the Cape during canola season, while blue hues are a spectacular sight up the West Coast and other farming areas during lupin season.

Canola fields, Overberg   55

Livestock

Bringing livestock to the Cape in limited cargo space was a problem Van Riebeeck knew he would have to bridge. He first tried to get cattle from the indigenous people, the *Strandlopers*, whom he encountered on his arrival, but they did not own cattle or breed livestock. He then began to barter with a tribe who lived close to where Saldanha Bay is today. They were not anxious to part with their livestock and as a result presented the animals that were in the poorest condition. These animals were easy targets, and predators and theft left a once big herd struggling to survive a few years later.

Van Riebeeck then moved the breeding programme to Robben Island where he also bred hares. He imported pigs and slowly began to supply meat to the passing ships, augmenting the availability with *dassies* (rock hyrax), seagulls and penguins. Penguin eggs became a delicacy and were readily available up to the 1950s.

Before long it was reported that sheep, cattle and milk cows were flourishing. Although great losses occurred initially, after two years of struggle the pioneer stockmen started winning the battle and an assortment of meats started appearing on the Cape table.

Herbs and spices were used generously to flavour local dishes, while oil and vinegar were imported and salt collected from the pans at the Salt River to use in meaty dishes. A true Cape innovation was to use rendered fat from fat-tailed sheep in cookery and this imparted a unique taste to local food.

The Tradition of the Braai

Although a lot of seafood is enjoyed by Capetonians today, another tradition reigns supreme – the *braai* (cooking meat on a metal grid over an open fire). This tradition epitomises Cape hospitality, and many a good laugh and meaningful conversation takes place around these fires.

Seafood, game, pork and poultry, along with things like vegetable kebabs, brown mushrooms and corn on the cob, end up on these grids. But the most popular of all are various cuts of beef (rump, sirloin, fillet and T-bone), *boerewors*, chicken and lamb chops. Bread rolls (called *roosterkoek* or grilled cakes) and various *sosaties* (kebabs) are regular features at a *braai*. The food has a smoky flavour when done this way.

The word *braai* (pronounced br-eye), or barbecue, conjures up more of a mood than a meal in South African parlance. A *braai* is a social event shared with family and friends around an open fire, and is usually handled by the men. Traditionally it is served with a few salads – usually potato salad and a fresh green salad. In winter, however, when it is cold, roasted vegetables or a potato bake is often served with the meat.

These meals tend to be casual and everyone helps themselves. Guests sit around the fire and eat on their laps, or around an informally laid table. Here are a few suggestions:

Lamb A popular marinade is a combination of lots of chopped garlic, fresh rosemary (leaves removed from the stalks and bruised slightly to release the flavour), olive oil and fresh lemon juice. The meat is left to marinate in this for at least an hour before the *braai*. It is best not to season the meat until it is almost cooked as the salt will toughen it. While on the grid, the meat is brushed with the marinade every so often.

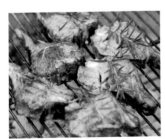

Chicken Chicken is best pre-cooked before going onto the grid, or it must be cooked very slowly and well. Use chicken portions and marinate as follows:

Pork As pork can be very dry, pork ribs and rashers are most popular. Brush with a mixture of olive oil and lemon juice while cooking. When cooked, season lightly with salt and pepper.

chicken marinade

METHOD
- Mix all the ingredients well.
- Place about 500 g chicken portions in a dish and pour the marinade over the chicken. Marinate for at least two hours – preferably more. Rotate the portions occasionally.
- Braai over mild coals and baste with the marinade every time you turn the portions over. The skin might look burnt but this is a result of the sugar in the tomato sauce.

INGREDIENTS
250 ml brown vinegar
250 ml sunflower oil
1 tbsp salt
2 tsp grated onion
1½ tsp mustard powder
62 ml tomato sauce
15 ml Worcester sauce
15 ml Tabasco sauce
2 tsp chopped garlic

Fish A fish *braai* is an art. Choose a fish – gutted, scaled and cleaned – with a firm flesh. Season with salt and pepper, baste with olive oil, and fill the cavity with slices of fresh lemon, thinly sliced onion and fresh basil or rosemary. Cook on both sides, over cooler coals, until the flesh is flaky. Baste with melted butter and freshly squeezed lemon juice every time it is turned over.

Beef A great idea is beef *sosaties* (kebabs), or cooking various cuts of steak.

Game Deboned leg or backstrap of game are good cuts to cook on the *braai*. Because game is also a dry meat, it is recommended that the meat be marinated for eight to 12 hours. On the next page is a good recipe for a marinade:

game marinade

INGREDIENTS

375 ml sunflower or canola oil
(not olive oil)
190 ml good quality dry
white wine
190 ml fruit juice like apricot
or grapefruit
4 large cloves of crushed garlic
zest and juice of 3 lemons
6 sprigs of rosemary
2 kg game meat, deboned and
sinews removed

Game done in this way is best served
medium-rare and thinly carved. Serve
with a cranberry jelly.

METHOD

• Mix the ingredients and pour over the meat, turning the meat to make sure all the sides are coated. Keep in a sealed container and leave in the refrigerator overnight, rotating a few times when possible.

• Before putting it on the grid, use a flour shaker and cover the entire piece of meat with a layer of flour. The flour forms a crust that seals the meat and keeps it succulent. While on the grid, continually baste with the remainder of the marinade and shake flour onto the meat with every basting. The last dredging of flour should take place no later than 10 minutes before the meat is removed from the fire or the flour will be uncooked. Season with salt and pepper at the last minute and serve immediately.

Potjiekos is a stew, usually with lamb, cooked in a three-legged cast iron pot on coals. The stew is cooked for hours, slowly over low heat, to allow all the flavours to mingle. This activity is a very social one that is enjoyed outdoors in sunny Cape Town.

roosterkoek
(bread rolls done over the coals)

METHOD

• Dissolve the dry yeast and honey in about one cup of the lukewarm water. Stir one tablespoon of the flour into this mixture, cover and leave in a draught-free spot for about five to 10 minutes to activate.

• Sift the remaining flour and salt into a mixing bowl. Make a hollow and add the yeast mixture. Mix and knead well until the dough is smooth. Add as much water as is needed gradually while kneading. Knead the soft butter into the mixture until it is evenly distributed.

• Cover with a dishcloth and place in a warm spot to rise to double its size. Then knock it back and form balls of about four centimetres in diameter. Place these on a lightly floured breadboard and flatten them a little. Cover with the dishcloth again and allow them to rise a little before placing the rolls on the grid. Place over coals of medium heat so as to cook the rolls and not burn them on the outside too quickly. Turn regularly until browned on both sides.

INGREDIENTS

2 tsp dry yeast
2 tsp honey
750 ml lukewarm water
1 kg flour
1 tsp salt
1 tbsp butter,
at room temperature

Serve hot with butter and various jams

Game

Although big game was plentiful in the early days, the settlers were unskilled at hunting at first. Their weapons were also not adequate. Gradually hunting game became popular, so much so that Lord Charles Somerset built a hunting lodge in a valley known as The Glen above Camps Bay. He acted as governor of the Cape colony during the mid-1800s and was a keen hunter. At this time venison was freely available and often found on the Cape table.

Hippo, Cape mountain zebra, *klipspringer* (rock jumper), *grysbok* (grey buck) and *duiker* (literally translated as diver – a reference to its diving motion as it moves through scrub) were found around Cape Town, and were plentiful. Today, due to urbanisation, only small game can be found on the mountains in more rural areas outlying Cape Town.

Game birds like helmeted guinea fowl, Cape spurfowl, wild duck and speckled (rock) pigeon are plentiful around Cape

Town, although not often used in our local cuisine. Cooking game birds is quite an art form and not too widely practised. Hunting speckled pigeons is very exciting as this coincides with strong south-easterly summer winds. The pigeons roost on the sides of Table Mountain as well as in the city centre. During the day they fly about 20 kilometres out of the city centre to feed on grain before starting the journey back in the afternoon, with the wind at their backs. It is said that they move at incredible speed, hugging the contours of the land, and so fly low and directly towards the guns – very challenging shooting.

There are a few game farms around Cape Town, as well as national parks, where game can be viewed. The *bontebok* (literally meaning buck with many colours), indigenous to the Western Cape, can also be seen in these parks and farms.

Delights from our Oceans

Meat and fresh produce was in short supply in the mid-1650s, so the early settlers turned to the ocean for their supply of protein – mostly in the form of fish and rock lobster. Records show that on the day after their arrival, Van Riebeeck sent sailors ashore to look for food. They caught no fewer than 750 *steenbras*, a fish that today is considered endangered.

The Dutch found the fish in the Cape waters to be delicious and they began to name them after species back home. The Cape *snoek*, a fish used in many a traditional dish, was named after a freshwater *snoek* found in the Netherlands. Rock lobster was plentiful and seafood became a significant part of local menus.

The Malay slaves changed the way seafood was prepared and many of the traditional fish dishes that are enjoyed at the Cape today are a result of the influence these creative people had on the development of a unique Cape cuisine. Rock lobster, abalone (*perlemoen*), periwinkles and limpets were commonplace. Today the harvesting of rock lobster and abalone is strictly monitored by law.

Black mussels can be picked off rocks along our coastline and fish and seafood are very much a staple part of our diet. Fish is prepared in a simple way, with the focus on the flavour and quality of the fish itself. Mussels are steamed, often in white wine, and served in a light creamy sauce. But many of the traditional ways of preparing fish are still widely practised, and dishes like fish cakes, *smoorsnoek* (*snoek* braised with onion and tomato) and pickled fish can be found both on restaurant menus and in home kitchens around the Cape. Pickled fish is made by cutting a fish like yellowtail or hake into cutlets, dipping these in egg and then coating them with flour. These cutlets are fried in oil in a pan, and placed into a curried sauce (see the recipe on page 148).

In this way, fish can be preserved a little longer than by keeping it fresh. The dish is so popular that some supermarkets sell it in their prepared meals section and many delis will have it in their cold displays.

The Atlantic Ocean is usually about 9°C colder than the Indian Ocean. This temperature difference, caused by the cold Benguela current that sweeps up from the Antarctic along the west coast, promotes a big diversity in marine life. This current also carries plankton, food for many fish species, which results in great fishing in the Atlantic Ocean.

On the eastern side, the Agulhas current, which flows from north to south, brings warmer waters preferred by whales and other marine life. The Southern Right whales arrive in this part of the ocean around July each year to birth their young and to breed. They have become a huge tourist attraction and can be seen at various points very close to the shoreline. In these warmer and safer waters, the young are birthed and helped along until they are strong enough to make the long journey back to the South Pole around November each year. Other whale species can also be seen but the Southern Right whales are predominant.

The colder waters of the Atlantic Ocean are better for rock lobster, periwinkles, black mussels, white mussels and oysters. Black mussel farming is practised in Saldanha Bay, so unless there is a red tide, mussels are available all year round.

Game fish, like *snoek*, tuna and yellowtail, are enjoyed regularly, as well as white-fleshed fish such as hake and kingklip.

Today our waters are monitored by SASSI (Southern African Sustainable Seafood Initiative) and consumers are informed via a comprehensive website regarding which species are plentiful and which are endangered.

Trout

Rainbow trout and, to a lesser degree, brown trout, were introduced to our rivers and have adapted well to Cape conditions. Fly-fishing has become popular and locals happily make the short trips out of town in various directions to pursue this passion in the Elandspad, Holsloot, Smalblaar and Witte rivers, mostly about an hour's drive from Cape Town. It has also become a popular tourist activity.

Up in the picturesque mountains near Franschhoek there is a trout farm that produces a range of trout products for the restaurant trade, as well as for retail, such as cold-smoked trout, hot-smoked trout and fresh trout fillets.

Dairy and Cheese

More than any other agricultural endeavour, dairy farming places the highest demand on staying abreast with technology. Because milk is perishable, and the industry is becoming less profitable, there is constant pressure on farmers to improve on quality and quantity. High-tech dairies yield milk for yoghurt, cheese and other dairy products.

This industry dates back to 1656 when the VOC granted Annetjie Boom (the wife of the head gardener at the Company's Garden) a lease for its cattle. In return she endeavoured to supply milk, butter and buttermilk to the local population, as well as to visitors at the Cape. From this small initiative, the dairy industry at the Cape has mushroomed, especially with regard to the quality and variety of cheese now produced.

At around this time the Dutch became leaders in cheese-making in Europe, and this art became one of the first industries to be launched at the Cape. Boom began making cottage cheese and as soon as the necessary equipment had arrived from the Netherlands, she added sweetmilk cheese and cumin cheese to her repertoire.

Today milk from cows, sheep, water buffalo and goats is used for cheese making and, in contrast to the mid-20th-century, the range of locally produced cheeses is enormous! Just about an hour's drive from Cape Town, outside the town of Wellington, the only *Mozzarella di Buffala* (an Italian-style mozzarella made using water buffalo milk) in South Africa is produced. Buffalo milk is lower in cholesterol and higher in calcium than cow's, goat's or sheep's milk.

Large-scale cheese producers share the stage with artisanal cheese makers, and together they are producing both traditional styles of cheeses and innovative creations that have added a unique flair to our cheese industry. Today the vast array of locally produced cheeses bears no resemblance to the limited selection of cheeses available in Cape Town even 30 years ago when a strong cheddar was considered avant-garde.

Baking

In 1659, when the governor first granted bakers permission to practise their trade, they began baking bread and pies. Fruit tarts made from apples and pears soon became a local favourite, and pies made from venison, chicken and lamb became Cape traditions. Pancakes and waffles were made in special long-handled irons over open fires and were served with honey and cream.

Probably the most famous pastry is the *koeksister*, for which the farming community and the Malay have different versions. The most accepted version, however, is that created by the Afrikaner farming community. A monument in Orania in the Northern Cape province of South Africa has even been built in its honour!

These pastries are such a part of our culture that a visit to the Cape would not be complete without sinking your teeth into at least one of them!

METHOD

- Prepare the syrup the day before.
- To make the syrup, place the sugar and water in a pot and stir over medium heat to dissolve the sugar. Add the cream of tartar, ginger and quills of cinnamon and allow to bubble away for five minutes. Add the glycerine just before the syrup is removed from the heat – this ensures a shiny look when the koeksisters are done.
- Place the syrup in the refrigerator and chill overnight.
- To make the dough, sift the dry ingredients together. Cut the cold butter into cubes and rub it into the flour mixture using your fingertips until it resembles breadcrumbs.
- Beat the egg, add the milk and add to the flour to form a soft dough. Knead well until the mixture is smooth and silky in texture. Cover with a dishcloth and set aside for two hours.
- Roll out the dough to a thickness of 1 cm and cut rectangles of about 6 x 10 cm. Lay the rectangles out in front of you lengthways and cut to form three strips from about 2 cm from the top of the rectangle. Braid the strips and press down at the end to seal.
- Heat the oil in a deep saucepan to a medium heat – the dough must brown slowly and not scorch on the outside while still raw on the inside.
- Deep-fry for one to two minutes until golden brown. Fry five to six at a time and allow one side to brown before flipping over to brown the other side. Remove from the oil using a slotted spoon and drain on paper towel for a few moments.
- Dunk them into the cold syrup and hold them down in the syrup for about a minute using a potato masher (if you leave them they will pop to the top and not absorb enough of the syrup).
- Remove from the syrup using a slotted spoon and place on a baking rack so that the surplus syrup drips off.

koeksisters

Makes 5 to 6 dozen

INGREDIENTS

4 cups flour
½ tsp salt
6 tsp baking powder
50 g butter
1 egg
125 ml milk
sunflower oil to fry in

For the syrup
4 cups sugar
375 ml water
½ tsp cream of tartar
½ tsp ground ginger
2 quills of cinnamon
2 tsp glycerine

Koeksisters keep very well. They can be frozen with great success and they defrost within minutes as they never freeze solidly due to the high sugar content.

Milk tart is another firm favourite in the Cape. The filling is flavoured with cinnamon and baked in the oven. Although there are a few versions, the basics remain the same.

Pancakes are South Africa's version of crêpes. They are slightly thicker and are traditionally sprinkled with cinnamon sugar and a dash of lemon juice and rolled up before serving. Many other variations on the theme have become vogue and savoury pancakes have also become very popular.

Today there are many artisanal bakers tantalising us with their fare around Cape Town. Josephine Mill, a water mill on the Liesbeek River at the foot of the eastern slopes of Table Mountain, is still operational and is producing stone-ground flour, as are other mills just outside of Cape Town.

Preserving

In the 17th and 18th centuries, housewives at the Cape were forced to exercise careful menu planning to ensure that there was never a shortage of produce to feed their families, and that whatever they had would not spoil.

To exacerbate this problem, the hot summers made it very difficult to preserve meat and these women were forced to develop methods of preservation. Out of necessity they began making *biltong* (similar to beef jerky).

The word *biltong* comes from the Dutch words *bil* (rump) and *tong* (tongue or strip). Biltong is made by cutting a thick flank of venison or beef into neat strips of about five centimetres wide and one-and-a-half centimetres thick, carefully removing sinews and tendons. Ostrich meat is often used as well. These strips are soaked in a vinegar solution for a day, then seasoned using spices like white pepper and coriander (usually the seeds, which are lightly toasted to release the flavour). They are then hung on hooks or from string, in a cool dry place, in such a way that the pieces don't touch. A fan is often placed in the room to help the drying process.

Smoking was and is another popular way of preserving both meat and fish. Other ways of preserving fish included salting, pickling and drying, all of which are still practised today. Smoked *snoek* is a very prominent feature on local menus.

Fruit and vegetables were also preserved to enjoy as an accompaniment to meat dishes. Fruit was mostly sundried, but also steeped in brandy. In the late 1700s, a Frenchman at the Cape discovered that fruit that was cooked in sugar and water, and stored in sterilised containers (these containers were steeped in boiling water), would last for a long time, provided these containers were not opened. Once opened, the contents had to be eaten fairly quickly. In this manner, jams and jellies were developed – the latter often serving as an accompaniment to meat dishes, especially game.

Although fresh produce is readily available these days, preserving is an art form still practised by many. Farm kitchens boast rows of jars filled with preserved fruit, jams and jellies. These jars act as trophies – a testament to the cook's reputation!

Olives and Olive Oil

Olive trees thrive in the local climate and generally do as well in similar conditions as vines. In and around the city, olive groves have produced top-class olives and olive oils.

Despite it being a young industry, our olive oils have reached the same standards as that of long-established olive oil-producing countries. Because of our latitude, the Cape is pressing olive oil in the European off-season and this creates a demand for our freshly pressed oils. International awards are abundant and we are carving out a prominent place in the global olive oil industry.

Berries

A few days after Van Riebeeck and his party arrived at the Cape, he sent a letter back to the Netherlands requesting that they send red, white and black currants, blackberries and dewberries to the Cape, where he thought they would adapt well. Initially this did not prove to be the case.

Much later, in the early 1920s, youngberries and boysenberries were produced commercially in Swellendam and used in the canning industry. Soon raspberries were grown in the Elgin district, most of which were exported to Covent Garden in London. Slowly this industry began to develop as Raymond O'Grady, who had studied in England in the mid-1970s, and who had become very interested in berries, began growing youngberries in his garden as a hobby.

When he moved house, he uprooted the canes (plants) and replanted them on a small farm outside Stellenbosch that he had just purchased. Here they thrived and soon so much was being harvested that he offered the surplus to the chef at Cape Town's iconic Mount Nelson Hotel, who eagerly accepted. O'Grady's journey took him abroad to learn more about berries and he brought his first raspberry and blackberry canes back with him. Twenty-five years ago, his business, Hillcrest Berry Orchards, became the first concern to sell a berry other than a strawberry into retail stores in the Cape.

New varieties are being developed all

the time to suit this region and lengthen the picking season. The Cape's winter rainfall climate is very favourable for berry growing. Berries love cold winters and although our climate is described as moderate, the winters are cold enough. But not so for the various currants – they need much colder conditions to thrive and have therefore never been grown here successfully. The picking season for the cane fruits begins in October and closes at the end of March/April. Commercially, the raspberry is the most popular local berry.

Cherries are grown in Ceres, about an hour's drive from Cape Town, and this season is the same as the strawberry season. Picking is also open to the public and this fun activity is enjoyed by many annually.

Strawberries are cultivated on a large scale around Stellenbosch where farmers have taken a fun approach to picking by opening up their farms to visitors. Scarecrows and giant strawberries beckon one to pull in, grab a container and get picking. Strawberry season is from October to January/February.

Apples and Pears

Although apricots and plums flourish in areas around Cape Town, apples and pears have become the most prominent of our deciduous export fruits.

They thrive in the Elgin valley, also about an hour's drive from Cape Town, which is significantly cooler than many surrounding areas.

Much of the apple and pear production is used to make juice. Apple juice in particular is used as a base for many other fresh fruit juices.

Apples are also used by the small but growing cider industry. Ciders were first introduced into South Africa in 1988 as an alternative to beer.

Table Grapes

Cape Town's climate is not optimal for table grapes which, to ensure a higher sugar content, need a hotter climate than the wine cultivars. But suitable varieties are cultivated a little further inland and yield significant quantities of high-quality table grapes for the export market.

Rumour has it that Jan van Riebeeck, the first Commander at the Cape, was responsible for the planting of *Hanepoot* grapes which, with its unique muscat character, has reserved a spot on the Cape table. Traditionally *Hanepoot* was used to make grape jam (*korrelkonfyt*) and today it can be used fresh with breadcrumbs, onion and herbs as a fragrant stuffing for chicken.

Hanepoot's other claim to fame is that in skilled hands it yields the most luscious of dessert wines.

Foraging

The *Strandlopers* (beach strollers) and the Bushmen (or San people) contributed to the early Cape menu by introducing the settlers to *veldkos* (edible wild plants at the Cape). Thankfully many of these plants are still known by the names they had back then. These people turned to nature for their food, and although these wild plants played an important role in the fight against scurvy among sailors, they initially played a secondary role in the diet of the European settlers.

Gradually the settlers learnt to prepare many plant species that appeared in the wild and today there is a growing resurgence of interest in foraging.

Waterblommetjies (pond blossoms)

This bulb grows in still, fresh water only in the Cape and the flowers are edible. They are harvested in the winter months by wading in the water – sometimes chest-deep – to pick the flowers. These are then rinsed well and can be used fresh in a stew, steamed as a vegetable or they can be blanched and frozen. *Waterblommetjie bredie* is a very traditional Cape dish.

The best months to enjoy these are July and August when the flower buds are still tender and at their plumpest.

Veldkool (wild asparagus)

This plant grows up the West Coast in sandy soil. Its name is derived from the fact that the tips resemble asparagus. It is only available for a short period of two to three weeks in mid-winter every year, and must be harvested before it begins to flower. It is delicious braised with onion and tomato or used in a stew.

Suurings (wild sorrel)

The stalks, rich in vitamin C, are sour and are traditionally used in a *waterblommetjie bredie* or in *veldkool* for a little acidity, which enhances both dishes. *Suurings* were initially used in place of lemons which were not available in the 1600s.

Chestnuts

Not indigenous to the Cape but available nevertheless, these give great delight to knowledgeable foragers.

Pine Nuts

With the introduction of pine trees from abroad came these wonderful edible seeds. Pine nuts are used in both sweet and savoury dishes. Traditionally they were used to make *tammeletjie* (stick-jaw).

Edible Mushrooms

Pine ring mushrooms (*Lactarius deliciosus*), with their creamy orange liquid when fried in butter, can be found growing in the carpet of fallen pine needles that cover the slopes around Cape Town.

Oaks were brought to the Cape in the late 1600s in an attempt to produce enough wood for vat production in a growing wine industry, and with them came the delights of various mushrooms from the *boletus* family, including the cep (also known as *porcini* or *boletus edulis*).

Chicken-of-the-woods *(laetiporus sulphureus)*, another edible fungus, grows on oaks and eucalyptus trees. This fungus has a different mouthfeel from traditional mushrooms and is bright yellow and orange in colour. Its lemony flavour adds a lovely tang to dishes.

There are other edible mushroom species, although the above-mentioned are the most common and popular.

Foraging for mushrooms is dangerous because some poisonous mushrooms can be mistaken for edible ones. So never attempt to forage without the accompaniment of someone in the know!

Wild Rosemary

Not as pungent as its relative, this plant occurs naturally as part of the Cape fynbos. It can be used in cooking, and its flavour is very subtle and slightly smoky.

Watercress

This plant, part of the nasturtium family, was found growing naturally beside running water in the Cape. Its peppery leaves add a delicious zing to salads.

Wild Figs

Two species of wild fig grow creeping on local sand dunes, and these succulent plants both produce edible fruit.

One is the sour fig, a gelatinous fruit that is used to make a preserve that is a wonderful accompaniment to cheese.

The other is called the Hottentot fig, after the tribe that introduced the settlers to this delicacy. The fruit of this plant is sweet and can be eaten fresh.

Buchu

Buchu is an indigenous herb. It is often used as an infusion for tea, and has many medicinal properties.

Rooibos Tea

Rooibos is a broom-like shrub, part of the fynbos. This plant, with its red needle-like leaves, is used to make a herbal tea that has become one of the Cape's trademarks. Although not technically a tea, the infusion made from oxidised leaves is commonly called tea. It is available in red and green varieties – the red colour the result of oxidation.

Traditionally it is enjoyed hot with a slice of lemon and honey, but iced tea and red espresso – the world's first tea espresso made from concentrated *rooibos* – are gaining popularity.

Rooibos tea has many health benefits. Firstly it contains no caffeine, and is filled with antioxidants, the most famous of which is Vitamin C. Tests have shown that it acts as an anti-inflammatory and has cardiovascular benefits.

Weather to go

The Cape climate may best be described as fickle Mediterranean – nothing is cast in stone, but there are trends. Changes in temperature and daylight hours lead to changes in what is available: the variety of fresh flowers, the fresh produce to be found, the menus that result from it and ultimately the mood of the city and its dwellers!

Summer, with its azure skies and oceans, is mostly dry and warm. The south-easterly wind keeps Cape Town's air clean and cools one down in temperatures that can reach 40°C plus on an extremely hot day. The beaches are crowded and picnics, *alfresco* dining and outdoor activities abound. Light fades around eight in the evening which makes for long, leisurely days.

Autumn, with its rich hues of golds, reds and oranges, is gaining a global reputation as a fine time to visit the city. Milder temperatures combined with still evenings create the right atmosphere for a *braai* beside the pool or at the beach. Sipping chilled wine and watching the orange orb disappear into the Atlantic Ocean at sunset is pure magic.

Winter is our rainy season but despite this, nothing beats a crisp, clear Cape Town winter's day. Roaring fireplaces greet one at many eateries, and this time of year is perfect for slow food and rich red wines. Snow falls on the mountain tops, but not to the extent found in the northern hemisphere. Vines are being pruned and primed for growth in spring.

With spring comes buds and blossoms and the countryside erupts in carpets of colour. Small shoots unfold into a vibrant green as ancient oaks and other trees push out their new leaves to greet the lengthening days. Fragrances cover the city like a light blanket.

The Cape as it Currently Captivates

More than ever before, contemporary Cape Town is a cosmopolitan city. Farming food production and urban food gardening are flourishing. And although one can find a restaurant to suit every palate, Cape hospitality in the home is better than ever.

This city and its surrounds have become a blank canvas where world-renowned chefs come to create their masterpieces using local and exotic ingredients. From fine dining restaurants – employing the most sophisticated aspects of the culinary arts – to humble wharf-side cafés and beach-side buffets where simple techniques yield a mouth-watering spectrum of fresh seafood and other fare, the Cape has it all. And there are restaurants in authentic historic settings where dishes that graced tables in the 1600s and 1700s can still be sampled, sometimes in the same buildings they were served in back then.

A growing profusion of markets serving freshly prepared foods as well as raw ingredients is popping up in and around the city. These markets have played a profound role in educating Capetonians in some unfamiliar produce such as Jerusalem artichokes and plantain, and a range of mushrooms, cheeses and breads.

It is here that expert chefs, innovative cooks and passionate producers can showcase their creations. These markets, ranging from sophisticated urban to rustic farm-style, have become a social event. Some specialise in organic fare only, while others cover a wide spectrum of produce from home kitchens and small businesses.

Various festivals mark the flow of each year. The Bastille Festival is celebrated on 14 July in Franschhoek. Crowds, garbed in their red, white and blue regalia, arrive in the village to indulge in traditional French diversions.

The Olive Festival in Riebeek Kasteel is celebrated early in May each year.

The South African Cheese Festival in Stellenbosch in April is another important date on the Cape culinary calendar.

The Good Food and Wine Show in May each year attracts foodies from around the country. Local and international celebrity chefs entertain passionate cooks, while specialised kitchen companies market the latest gadgets.

As Cape Town has always been all about producing food, one can only imagine that the excitement at these events is similar to that of the atmosphere at the early market held at Greenmarket Square.

Because of our moderate climate, a lot of dining is done *alfresco* for the greater part of the year. And, latterly, more than ever before, there is a local wine to be paired perfectly with any dish. Some of the world's top restaurants are located in Cape Town and they and their chefs feature routinely on the lists of top restaurants in the world.

The Cape Town of the mid-17th-century was developed around the need for fresh produce and soon it became a popular travel destination where food was celebrated and written about. That trend is still alive.

Cape cuisine remains a fusion of styles and flavours of the various cultures that call this home – a Rainbow Nation indeed.

Conclusion

Today a rich tapestry of local recipes graces our tables at the Cape. Like a fine blended wine, Cape cuisine offers complexity, richness and a host of subtle and exotic nuances to delight the most discerning and adventurous of palates.

For more than three centuries, the Cape has continued to provide for the needs of visitors from all parts of the world, making it truly worthy of its title of old, Tavern of the Seas.

We now invite you on a journey into a Cape kitchen, and trust you will enjoy what we have prepared for you!

recipes

beetroot pancakes

INGREDIENTS

1 small beetroot, cooked
1 cup flour
250 ml milk
3 eggs
15 ml oil
¼ tsp salt
¼ tsp baking powder
sunflower oil to fry in
2 tsp ground cinnamon
4 tbsp sugar
12 Adam's figs
250 ml double thick fresh cream
50 ml raw honey

METHOD

• In a processor, blend the beetroot, flour, milk, eggs, oil, salt and baking powder until smooth. Pour into a bowl and leave to rest for at least an hour.

• Use a non-stick frying pan to make thin pancakes. Fry in a drizzle of oil.

• Mix the cinnamon and sugar, and sprinkle over the hot pancakes before rolling them up. Serve with fresh Adam's figs, a blob of double thick cream and a drizzle of raw honey.

Never top and tail a beetroot – cook whole and do not break the skin. Keep at least 5 cm of the stalk intact – it will stop the colour bleeding during the cooking process. The beets are cooked when the skin peels away easily.

A colourful twist to an ol

avourite

biltong and peppadew™ roll

Serves 8 to 10

METHOD

• Place a sheet of cling flim on a flat working surface. Place 3 rows of biltong in rows to measure a rectangle of 15 x 25 cm, and press down. Spread evenly with cottage cheese. Top with a row of Peppadews™ about 5 cm from the bottom.

• Place both hands under the cling flim and fold it from the bottom towards the centre. Peel the cling flim back to rest on the working surface. Fold the top over to the centre in the same way. Carefully fold the bottom cling flim over the roll and fold the sides in. Mould into a tight sausage shape with both hands. Refrigerate overnight.

• Remove from the plastic and slice into rounds of about 1½ cm in thickness using a sharp knife.

• Serve as a starter on some watercress or as a snack on a cracker.

INGREDIENTS

3 cups moist beef biltong, thinly sliced
300 g smooth cottage cheese
1 cup Peppadews™, drained

Uniquely South African ingredients

You can replace the biltong with roasted red peppers, and the Peppadews™ with pitted olives. The above ingredients are very typically South African, but might not be readily available. I also sometimes add coarsely chopped rocket on to the cottage cheese for more colour and serve it with avocado on lettuce.

Traditional Cape Malay cuisine

bobotie

METHOD

- Preheat the oven to 180°C.
- Heat the oil in a saucepan and fry the onions until cooked. Add the garlic and cook until transparent. Sprinkle the curry powder over the onions, add the salt and stir, allowing the heat to release the flavours. Then add the mince and stir until cooked.
- Pour in the vinegar and cover with the lid – cook together for 15 minutes. Add the turmeric to the meat mixture and stir through. Soak the bread in milk and remove. Squeeze the excess milk out and mash with a fork. Add the soggy bread to the meat mixture and add the beaten egg. Stir with a wooden spoon until mixed well.
- Add the smooth apricot jam, the raisins, the apricots and the apple and stir them into the mixture.
- Place the cooked mince in a buttered pie dish. Lay the bay leaves on top of the mince.
- To make the topping, add the 2 eggs to the yoghurt and cream and season with a pinch each of salt and cayenne pepper. Beat until mixed well. Pour over the top of the meat.
- Bake for 40 minutes or until the custard sets on top.

Cooked bobotie freezes very well. This dish is synonymous with Cape Malay cooking. It is traditionally an aromatic beef dish but can also be made using ground ostrich, lamb, chicken, fish. For a vegetarian option use lentils.

INGREDIENTS

30 ml olive oil
2 onions, sliced
2 cloves garlic, crushed
2 tbsp curry powder, medium strength
1 tsp salt
1 kg ground (minced) meat – beef
or ostrich or lamb
15 ml vinegar
2 thick slices white bread, crusts removed
milk to soak the bread in
2 tbsp turmeric
1 egg, beaten
2 tbsp smooth apricot jam
a handful of raisins
a few soft, dried apricots,
cut into quarters
1 Granny Smith apple, peeled and
coarsely grated
bay leaves

Topping
2 eggs
125 ml plain yoghurt
125 ml cream
1 pinch salt
1 pinch cayenne pepper

boerewors and nectarine salad

Serves 4 to 6

METHOD

• Heat 1 teaspoon olive oil in a non-stick pan and cook the sausage until brown. Remove from the pan and cut into bite-sized chunks.

• Toast the almond flakes in a dry pan until golden brown. Remove from the heat and allow to cool.

• Toss the butter lettuce in olive oil and place on a platter. Cut the nectarines into slices and place on the lettuce leaves.

• Top with the boerewors chunks and the pomegranate arils. Drizzle with a little olive oil and a dash of balsamic glaze and scatter the roasted almond flakes on top.

.

INGREDIENTS

olive oil
250 g boerewors
50 g almond flakes
300 g butter lettuce
2 ripe nectarines, stones removed
arils of half a pomegranate
balsamic glaze

There are as many boerewors recipes as there are boerewors makers, and all of them keep their versions close to their chests!

cabbage frikkadels

INGREDIENTS

1 whole cabbage
350 g minced lamb
½ cup basmati rice
1 small onion, chopped
salt and pepper to season
a sprinkling of nutmeg
1 small onion, cut into quarters
2 gloves of garlic, peeled
400 g chopped tomatoes in
tomato sauce
250 ml water
more salt, about ½ tsp

METHOD

• Peel off the leaves of the cabbage, keeping them whole and carefully remove the thick part at the base of the spine by cutting it out in a V-shape – a maximum of 5 cm long.

• Mix the raw minced lamb and the raw basmati rice with the chopped onion and season with the salt, pepper and nutmeg.

• Place the cabbage leaves in a bowl of boiling water to soften them, one at a time, until they are pliable.

• Form a sausage shape with the meat mixture, about the size of half a banana. Place it sideways on a cabbage leaf, perpendicular to the central spine of the leaf (nearest to the V) and begin rolling by folding the flaps on either side of the V over the meat and rolling them another time to secure. Fold the sides of the cabbage in snugly and roll all the way to the end. Repeat until you have used up all the meat.

• Place the cabbage rolls in the bottom of a saucepan. Place the quartered onion in the saucepan along with the garlic cloves, chopped tomatoes and water. Add the extra salt and bring to the boil. Simmer for about 45 minutes until the rice is tender and the flavours have mingled.

• Serve with roasted vegetables or on its own as a starter.

The nutmeg in this dish enhances the flavou

fish cakes

INGREDIENTS

750 g white-flesh fish, filleted,
cleaned and skinned
juice of 1 lemon
200 g potatoes, peeled and
steamed until soft
2 spring onions, finely chopped
20 g chives, finely chopped
10 g dill, finely chopped
salt and freshly milled black pepper
to season
a generous sprinkling of nutmeg
a sprinkling of dried chillies
oil to fry the fish cakes in

METHOD

• Preheat the oven to 180°C.
• Place the fish fillets in an ovenproof dish, squeeze the lemon juice over the fish and place the squeezed lemons on top. Cover with foil and bake in the oven for about 20 minutes or until cooked.
• Take the dish out of the oven and remove the fish from the liquid. Set aside to cool a little and then flake the flesh, making sure all the bones have been removed.
• Mash the potatoes coarsely. Add the spring onions, the chives, the dill and the potato to the fish and mix. Season with salt, pepper, nutmeg and chillies. Mix well and allow to rest in the refrigerator for an hour.
• Remove from the refrigerator and form cakes of about 8 cm wide and 2 cm thick. Heat the oil in a frying pan and fry until golden brown on both sides.
• Serve with mayonnaise or tartar sauce and a fresh green salad.

These can be prepared in advance and
cooked just before serving.

ginger beer

Makes 4½ litres

INGREDIENTS

4 cups sugar
1 tsp tartaric acid
1 tsp cream of tartar
4½ litres warm water
4 tsp Jamaica ginger
1 tsp ground ginger and a little cold water to form a paste

For the yeast
3 tsp sugar
125 ml lukewarm water
2 tsp dry yeast

METHOD

• Mix the ingredients for the yeast in a cup and leave in a warm place to activate.

• Mix the sugar, tartaric acid, cream of tartar and warm water in a large container and stir until the sugar has dissolved. Add the Jamaica ginger and the ground ginger paste and stir.

• Add the yeast and mix well. Allow to cool.

• Pour the ginger beer into 1-litre bottles and refrigerate.

• Serve chilled.

This recipe can be prepared in large quantities and kept refrigerated for a long time.

This chutney will also go well with curry o

ginger, pear and carrot chutney

Makes 5 cups (1250 ml)

INGREDIENTS

5 medium-sized pears, peeled, cored and diced
2 onions, finely diced
¾ cup sultanas
1 quill of cinnamon
1 tbsp grated fresh ginger
1 tsp mustard seeds
375 ml cider vinegar
1½ cups treacle sugar
1 tsp salt
4 medium-sized carrots, peeled and coarsely grated

METHOD

• Place all the ingredients, except the carrots, in a saucepan and bring to the boil, stirring until the sugar dissolves. Turn the heat down and simmer on medium for 30 minutes.

• Sterilise the jars by washing them in hot, soapy water, rinsing them well and placing them in a preheated oven at 160°C for 20 minutes.

• Add the carrots and reduce the heat to low – simmer for another 30 minutes until the liquid has reduced and the mixture has thickened. Remove the quill of cinnamon.

• Ladle the hot chutney into the jars and seal well. Store in a cool, dark place for at least two weeks for the flavours to develop. If sterilised, sealed and stored properly, chutney can last up to 12 months. Refrigerate after opening.

• Serve with a strong cheese and a crusty loaf.

obotie

Malay cooking incorporates sweet with savoury.

guineafowl samoosas

Makes about 100 samoosas

METHOD

• Heat the oil in a heavy-bottomed saucepan. Add the quartered onion and fry until transparent. Add the guineafowl and brown that together with the onion. Add the bay leaves, peppercorns, juice, stock, wine, garlic and carrots and simmer for 2 hours until tender.

• Preheat the oven to 180°C.

• Set aside to cool before carefully removing the meat from the bones, making sure that – if this is not a domesticated bird – all pellets are removed. This is a delicate procedure.

• When all the meat has been removed, place it in a dish and add some of the mixture and juice from the saucepan to moisten it without making it too runny (as this will make the pastry go soggy).

• Lay the phyllo pastry sheets out on a clean surface and be sure to cover what is not being used at the time with a damp kitchen cloth to prevent it from drying out.

• Use the diagram to fold the samoosas, adding a heaped teaspoon of the filling to each. Brush with the melted butter, making sure you brush everywhere. Place on a baking tray lined with baking paper and bake until golden brown. Serve immediately, 3 to 4 per person, with sour fig preserve.

The filling can be frozen successfully and defrosted when needed. These little triangular pastries can also be filled with something sweet like a mixture of honey, butter, spices and nuts.

INGREDIENTS

45 ml olive oil to fry the onion in
1 large onion, quartered
1 guineafowl of about 1 kg, skinned
2 bay leaves
4 whole black peppercorns
500 ml apricot juice
500 ml chicken stock
500 ml good quality dry white wine
1 whole clove of garlic, peeled
200 g carrots julienne
phyllo pastry
100 g butter, melted

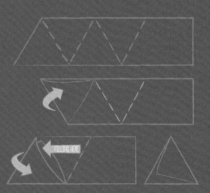

health rusks

INGREDIENTS

700 g butter
875 ml buttermilk
500 g sugar
4 eggs
1 packet (400 g) Kellogg's Honey
and Nut Flakes
1 packet (400 g) Kellogg's All Bran
with Berries
100 g unsalted hazel nuts, crushed
200 g unsalted cashew nuts, crushed
200 g unsalted almonds, crushed
100 g sundried cranberries
100 g dried, diced apple
50 g toasted sesame seeds
1 tbsp ground cinnamon
1 tbsp ground pimento allspice
1 tbsp ground mixed spice
a sprinkling of freshly
ground nutmeg
1½ kg self-raising flour
10 tsp baking powder
1½ tsp salt

METHOD

• Preheat the oven to 180°C.
• Grease ovenproof dishes or bread tins and set aside.
• Melt the butter in quite a large pot. Remove from the heat and use a whisk to beat in the buttermilk, sugar and eggs. Mix well.
• Mix the rest of the ingredients together in a big mixing bowl. I crush the bran flakes a little so that it is easier to mix. Add the butter mixture to the dry ingredients and mix well using a wooden spoon. The mixture will be loose and sticky.
• Form balls of about the size of an apricot and pack them tightly together in the greased ovenproof dishes. Place in the oven and bake for between 45 minutes and 1 hour, or until cooked through. Remove from the oven and allow to cool.
• Break into rusk-sized portions, i.e. 5 x 2½ cm. Place the rusks on an oven rack and leave in the oven overnight at 70°C to dry out, with the door slightly ajar (so that all the moisture can escape.)
• Enjoy by dunking into coffee or tea.

There is nothing as good as dunking a rusk into one's firs

up of morning coffee

chicken pies

METHOD

• For the filling, brown the onion in the olive oil in a large pot. Add the whole chicken and brown on all sides. Add the thyme, the lemon juice, the wine and the stock and simmer for 1 hour. Set aside to cool.

• Remove the flesh from the bones and chop into bite-sized chunks.

• In a separate pot, brown the leeks in the olive oil. Add the chicken, nutmeg, salt and pepper, and enough of the stock to make the filling moist but not too wet. Set the filling aside to cool completely before continuing.

• Preheat the oven to 200°C.

• Roll out the pastry on a lightly-floured surface to a thickness of about 5 mm. Lightly grease a big muffin tray with melted butter. Cut the pastry into 12 rounds to fit into the individual compartments. Press these down to cover the surface and up the sides. Cut out another 12 circles of pastry to use as lids.

• Spoon the cooled chicken filling into each pie shell. You can heap it before covering with the reserved pastry rounds. Use your fingertips to press down around the edges to secure the lids to the rest of the pastry.

• Brush the pastry with the beaten egg and then bake the pies for 15 to 20 minutes or until golden brown.

INGREDIENTS

2 medium-sized onions, cut each into eighths
45 ml olive oil (plus 45 ml to brown the leeks)
1 whole free-range chicken of about 1.2 kg
a bunch of fresh thyme
juice of 2 lemons
150 ml dry white wine
200 ml chicken stock
400 g leeks, thinly sliced
¼ tsp ground nutmeg
2 tsp salt
freshly milled black pepper to taste
1 roll (400 g) ready-made puff pastry
2 tbsp butter, melted
1 egg, beaten

Serve hot with a salad or vegetables. These can also be made into one large pie.

jan smuts cookies

INGREDIENTS

400 g all-purpose flour
10 ml baking powder
a generous pinch of salt
250 g butter, at room temperature
200 g sugar
2 eggs, beaten

Filling
125 g butter at room temperature
125 g sugar
2 eggs, beaten
125 g all-purpose flour
1 tsp baking powder
100 ml fine smooth apricot jam

General Jan Smuts was a prominent South African and British Commonwealth statesman, military leader and philosopher. His views were more liberal than that of his successor, General JBM Hertzog, and so the country became divided behind these two figures. Two versions of a similar recipe were developed, one called Jan Smuts cookies and the other Hertzoggies, as a testament to this divide.

METHOD

• Preheat the oven to 190°C.
• Spray 3 x 12 small muffin trays with a non-stick spray.
• Sift the flour, baking powder and salt together. Rub the butter into the dry ingredients using your fingertips until the mixture resembles fine crumbs. Add the sugar and mix. Add the eggs, one at a time, and mix until a dough forms.
• Roll the dough out to a thickness of about 3 mm on a cool surface that has been lightly sprinkled with flour. Cut circles of about 8 cm in diameter using a cookie cutter. Line the hollows of the muffin tray with the circles of dough.
• To make the filling, cream the butter and sugar together. Add the eggs one at a time, mixing well between each addition. Sift the flour and baking powder together and add to the egg mixture. Mix well.
• Place half a teaspoon of smooth apricot jam into each hollow of the lined muffin trays. Top with a tablespoonful of the filling.
• Bake for 15 minutes or until golden brown. Remove from the oven and turn them onto a steel rack to cool.
• Store in an airtight container.

lamb loin chops on the braai

Serves 6

METHOD

• Mix the olive oil, garlic, lemon juice and rosemary in a flat dish. Place the lamb chops in the dish, coating both sides with the mixture. Allow the meat to marinate for about an hour.

• In the meanwhile, light your fire using either wood or briquettes (you may use a gas barbecue) and when the coals are glowing, allow them to burn out a little so that your fire is not too hot.

• Line the chops up in the same direction on a skewer and begin the cooking process with the long bone facing towards the coals. When that has browned, turn the chops onto their fatty side. The fat may cause the flames to flare up so be careful not to let the fat burn.

• While on the grid, brush with the marinade every so often. Cook the meat on the fatty side until the fat has dripped off and is crispy. Turn the meat on to the final side and cook until browned. The chops are now cooked on three sides.

• Finally, remove them from the skewers and cook briefly on both flat sides until they are at rare, medium or well-done stage, whichever you prefer.

• Season with salt and pepper and a dash of freshly squeezed lemon juice before serving. Meat done over the coals is best enjoyed immediately.

INGREDIENTS

75 ml olive oil
3 large cloves garlic, crushed
juice of 1 lemon
(plus extra for seasoning)
3 sprigs of rosemary,
leaves removed from the stalks,
and bruised to release the flavour
12 lamb loin chops
of about 2 cm in thickness
salt and freshly milled black pepper

On the 24th of
September we
celebrate
National Braai Day

malay chicken curry

Serves 4 to 6

INGREDIENTS

60 ml olive oil
2 medium onions, sliced
2 cloves garlic, chopped
2 tbsp curry powder, medium strength
¼ tsp fresh ginger, grated
3 cinnamon quills
2 bay leaves
2 medium tomatoes, peeled and chopped
8 chicken portions
60 ml water
salt and freshly milled black pepper to taste
100 g soft dried apricots
125 g dried prunes, pitted

METHOD

• Heat the olive oil in a saucepan. Fry the onions until they start to go brown. Add the garlic and continue to fry, being careful not to allow the garlic to go brown. Add the curry powder, ginger, cinnamon quills and bay leaves and fry to release the flavours. Add the chopped tomatoes and fry lightly.

• Place the chicken portions in the saucepan, and then the water. Cover and cook slowly for about 30 minutes.

• Season with salt and pepper and add the dried fruit.

• Cover again and cook slowly for a further hour.

• Serve on a bed of basmati rice with sweet pumpkin and greens.

This aromatic dish can also be prepared using lamb neck or knuckles.

Mala

rries are traditionally spicy and sweet rather than hot

This baked dessert gets its name from it

malva pudding

Serves 8

METHOD

- Preheat the oven to 180°C.
- Beat the egg, sugar and jam together on high for about 15 minutes. Sift the flour, bicarbonate of soda and salt into a bowl.
- Melt the butter and add the vinegar. Set aside.
- Add the milk and cream to the egg mixture, alternating with the flour mixture. Finally add the vinegar and butter and mix well.
- Pour the batter into a dish of approximately 20 x 30 cm, and cover with foil. Bake for 45 minutes to 1 hour until it has a consistent rich brown colour.
- Melt the ingredients for the sauce in a saucepan so that it is ready when the pudding comes out of the oven. Carefully pour it over the pudding, one cup at a time, until it has been absorbed.
- This pudding is best served warm so either cover with the foil again or reheat in the oven.
- Serve with fresh berries and custard.

INGREDIENTS

1 egg
1 cup sugar
1 tbsp smooth apricot jam
1 cup flour
1 tsp bicarbonate of soda
a generous pinch of salt
1 tbsp butter
5 ml white vinegar
125 ml milk
125 ml cream

Sauce
125 ml milk
125 ml cream
180 g butter
1 cup sugar
125 ml hot water

milarity in texture to marshmallows (malva in Afrikaans)

milk tart

INGREDIENTS

3 tbsp sugar
1 tbsp flour
1 tbsp cornflour
375 ml milk
1 quill of cinnamon
1½ tbsp butter
a generous pinch of salt
2 eggs, separated
1 roll (400 g) ready-made
puff pastry

METHOD

• Preheat the oven to 180°C.
• Mix the sugar, flour and cornflour to a paste with a little of the milk. Scald (heat gently, do not allow to boil) the remaining milk with the quill of cinnamon and add the cornflour mixture. Return the mixture to the saucepan and cook for 15 minutes, stirring until thick and smooth. Remove from the heat and stir in the butter. Set aside to cool.
• When the mixture is cool, add the egg yolks, one at a time, mixing well. Add the salt and mix well.
• Whisk the egg whites until soft peaks form and fold gently into the custard.
• Line a 20 cm tart dish with puff pastry and pour the mixture into the dish.
• Bake for 20 minutes or until evenly golden brown on top.

There is also a version of this old favourite that is served as a refrigerated tart.

Milk tart is another firm favouri

B. RADEMEYER

ZWARTKOPS
DAIRY/MELKERY

PHONE/FOON 18

the Cape

naartjie (tangerine) granita

Makes about 200 ml

INGREDIENTS
12 naartjies (tangerines), cut in half and juiced
1 tsp lemon verbena, finely chopped

METHOD
• Mix the lemon verbena into the juice and place the mixture in a shallow dish. Place the dish in the freezer and leave until crystals begin to form. Break the crystals by stirring with a spoon and leave again for another 30 minutes. Repeat the process until the crystals are small and flaky.

• Serve as a palate cleanser between courses.

The flavour of this citrus fruit is synonymous with Cape Town

ostrich fillet with onion marmalade

Serves 4

METHOD

- To prepare the marmalade, fry the onions in the butter until they begin to brown. Add the red wine, the port and the red wine vinegar and bring to the boil. When reduced by a third, add the honey and continue to cook covered for about 1 hour until concentrated and sticky.
- Melt the butter and oil in a heavy-bottomed pan and sear the fillets until golden brown on each side. Remove from the heat when cooked to your liking and allow to rest (Ideally ostrich is enjoyed rare or medium-rare).
- Steam the potatoes for about 20 minutes or until soft. Place in a dish and mash using a hand masher. Heat the milk and the butter and pour over the potatoes and mix well. Add the crushed garlic and blend it into the fluffy potatoes. Season with salt and nutmeg.
- To serve, place a bed of mashed potato on each plate and top with the sliced ostrich fillet and some of the onion marmalade. Serve with seasonal vegetables.

INGREDIENTS

Onion marmalade
3 medium-sized onions, finely sliced
3 tbsp butter
100 ml good quality red wine
100 ml port
100 ml red wine vinegar
45 ml honey

Ostrich
4 x 200 g ostrich fillets
1 tsp butter
10 ml oil
salt and freshly milled black pepper
to season

Garlicky mashed potatoes
4 large potatoes, peeled and cubed
100 ml full cream milk
2 tbsp butter
1 large clove of garlic, peeled and
crushed
salt to season
a sprinkling of nutmeg

Ostrich meat contains very little fat

oxtail stew

Serves 6 to 8

METHOD

• Trim the excess fat from the meat. Season the flour with the salt, pepper, cayenne pepper and mustard powder and toss the meat in the flour.

• Heat the butter and olive oil in a large pan over moderate heat and seal the meat, turning until the pieces are golden brown on all sides. In a separate large pot, heat the oil and fry the onions until brown. Add the carrots, celery and garlic and fry for a few more minutes.

• Place the oxtail in the pot and pour the wine over the dish. Tuck the bay leaves, orange zest and thyme in between the joints of the meat.

• Cover and simmer for 2½ hours, turning the meat over every hour. Remove the meat from the pot and skim the fat off the top of the sauce. Turn up the heat and allow the juices to reduce for 30 minutes. Place the meat back into the pot and add the baby potatoes. Cook for another 30 minutes until the potatoes are tender.

• Serve with basmati rice.

INGREDIENTS

1.8 kg oxtail, cut into joints
½ cup flour for dusting the joints
salt and freshly milled black pepper
to season
a generous pinch of cayenne pepper
1 tsp mustard powder
2 tbsp butter
45 ml olive oil (plus a little extra for
frying the onions)
3 onions, peeled and quartered
6 carrots, peeled and
cut into chunks
3 celery sticks, coarsely chopped
1 head of garlic, whole,
but with the tops chopped off
2 bay leaves
1 bottle (750 ml) Merlot
zest of 1 orange
bunch of fresh thyme
10 baby potatoes, peeled

This stew gets better with time and can be prepared a day in advance with great success. Leave it overnight in the refrigerator.

pine nut and honey tart

INGREDIENTS

1 roll (400 g) ready-made
shortcrust pastry
250 g pine nuts
250 g butter
250 g sugar
a pinch of salt
60 ml honey
3 whole eggs
115 g flour
a handful of thyme
zest of 1 orange
crème fraîche to serve

METHOD

• Preheat the oven to 180°C.

• Line a 30 cm tart ring with the pastry and prick the pastry base with a fork. Place in the oven and bake for 10 minutes at 180°C. Remove from the oven and set aside. Reduce the heat to 170°C.

• Lightly toast the pine nuts in a pan. Allow to cool.

• Cream the butter, sugar, salt and honey together until light and fluffy. Add the eggs, one at a time, and mix well. Add the flour and mix lightly. Finally add the pine nuts, thyme and orange zest and mix together by hand.

• Pour into the tart dish and place in the oven for 35 minutes. Remove from the oven and set aside to cool.

• Serve at room temperature with a dollop of crème fraîche.

The pine forests on the slopes of Table Mountain have been the source not only of these seeds but also of pine ring mushrooms

cape pickled fish

INGREDIENTS

750 g yellowtail cutlets (can
be substituted with hake)
flour for dusting
sunflower oil for frying

Curry sauce
2 large onions, sliced into thin rings
375 ml brown or white vinegar
250 ml water
1½ cups brown or white sugar
1 tbsp curry powder,
medium strength
1 tsp turmeric
¼ tsp allspice, ground
1 tsp salt
thumb-sized piece of fresh ginger,
peeled and cut into thin slices
10 black peppercorns
3 juniper berries, dried
4 curry leaves
3 tbsp cornflour, mixed with 45 ml
water to form a smooth paste

METHOD

• Wash the fish and make sure all the scales and bones
have been removed. Pat dry using paper towel.

• Dust the fish lightly with flour and set aside.

• In a large saucepan combine all the curry sauce
ingredients, except the cornflour paste, and bring to the
boil. Simmer vigorously and uncovered for 5 minutes. Add
the cornflour paste to the sauce and stir until the sauce
thickens. Simmer for another 5 minutes.

• Remove from the heat and place the lid on the saucepan
to keep the sauce warm.

• Heat the oil in a pan and fry the fish until cooked. Place
the hot fish in a glass dish and pour the hot sauce over the
cutlets. Allow to cool before covering and placing in the
refrigerator.

• Serve cold or at room temperature with a crusty seed
loaf.

This dish is best eaten after a day or two and can keep up to a week
in the refrigerator.

Traditionally served as ar

pumpkin fritters

Serves 6 to 8

METHOD

• Steam the pumpkin for about 40 minutes or until tender. Set aside to cool a little before mashing it using a fork.

• Mix the ready-cooked pumpkin, baking powder, flour, salt and eggs together. Let it stand for 10 minutes or more or you may leave it overnight. If the mixture is a bit runny add more flour.

• Cover the base of a frying pan with oil and bring to a medium heat. Place tablespoonfuls of batter into the hot oil and fry until golden brown on both sides. Drain on a paper towel.

• Stack 3 on top of one another with a blob of crème fraîche in between. Drizzle with honey and dust with cinnamon. Serve warm or hot.

INGREDIENTS

500 g raw pumpkin, peeled and diced (need 2 cups ready-cooked pumpkin)
1 tbsp baking powder
¾ cup flour
½ tsp salt
2 eggs
vegetable oil for frying

Topping
2 tsp cinnamon
honey
crème fraîche

accompaniment to the main course

Pumpkin fritters freeze well. Reheat in a frying pan before serving.

roly-poly pudding

INGREDIENTS
2 cups flour
2 tsp baking powder
125 g butter, cold and cubed
2 eggs, beaten
milk, about 62 ml
smooth apricot jam

Syrup
375 ml boiling water
1 cup sugar
2 tbsp butter

METHOD
• Preheat the oven to 180°C.
• Sift the flour and baking powder together. Rub the butter into the dry ingredients. Add the beaten eggs and just enough milk to form a stiff dough.
• Roll out the dough into a rectangular shape as thinly as possible. Spread the surface with a thin layer of apricot jam. Roll the rectangle into a long shape and cut into wheels of about 1 cm thick. Place snugly together in an oven dish.
• Make the syrup by mixing all the ingredients together and stirring until the sugar has dissolved. Pour the syrup over the wheels and place in the oven. Bake for about 1 hour until golden brown and sticky.
• Serve with custard.

You can bake this dessert ahead of time. To serve, drizzle with a little boiling water and warm in a preheated oven.

seed loaf

Makes 1 large loaf

METHOD

• Preheat the oven to 200°C.

• Mix all the dry ingredients together (except the seeds) and then add the water and the oil. Mix well: the consistency should be soft, not runny.

• Brush a bread tin lightly with butter. Spoon the dough into the tin and sprinkle the seeds on top – I use a mixture of linseed, poppy seeds, sesame seeds and sunflower seeds. Cover with a clean dish towel and allow the loaf to rise in a warm place for 1 hour, away from a draft.

• Place in the oven and bake for 1 hour. Tip the hot loaf out onto a steel rack immediately and do not cover – this will result in a crunchy loaf.

INGREDIENTS

6 cups Nutty Wheat flour
2 tsp instant yeast
1 tbsp salt
1 tbsp treacle sugar
690 ml warm water
30 ml sunflower oil
mixed seeds

nutty and textured

Creamy onion sala

slaphakskeentjies

Serves 12

• Bring the salted water to the boil in a large pot. Add the onions to the boiling water and cook for about 10 minutes or until they are just cooked. The onions should still be firm. Drain and set aside while you prepare the creamy sauce.

• Bring a small pot of water to the boil.

• Beat the eggs in a metal container and add the sugar. Beat for a few minutes before adding the vinegar and the water. Place the metal container with the mixture over the pot with boiling water and stir continuously for about 5 to 7 minutes until it thickens.

• Pour the warm sauce over the onions and allow to cool. This dish can keep in the refrigerator for a week or it can be stored in airtight sterilised containers. Serve with braaivleis.

3½ litres water with 2 tbsp sea salt to cook the onions in
1½ kg pickling onions, peeled
4 eggs
4 tbsp sugar
60 ml white grape vinegar
60 ml water

ade using pickling onions

This salad got its name because the small onions resemble the ball joint of the heel of an animal. Literally translated from Afrikaans it means 'little floppy heels'.

smoked snoek pâté

INGREDIENTS

250 g smoked snoek
150 ml crème fraîche
30 ml fresh cream
125 g butter, soft
the juice and rind of 1 lemon
freshly milled black pepper to
season
4 spring onions, finely chopped
1 tbsp chopped capers
1 tbsp chopped chives
1 tbsp chopped parsley

METHOD

• Shred the snoek using your fingers and make sure to remove all the bones. Place in the bowl of a food processor.
• Add the crème fraîche, cream, butter, rind of the lemon and the lemon juice, and season with the freshly milled black pepper. Process until smooth.
• Add the spring onions, capers, chives and parsley and mix this into the smooth snoek mixture.
• Place the pâté in a bowl and smooth the surface. Serve with a crusty seed loaf.

Snoek is a game fish with firm flesh commonly found in our waters and is often used in

variety of dishes

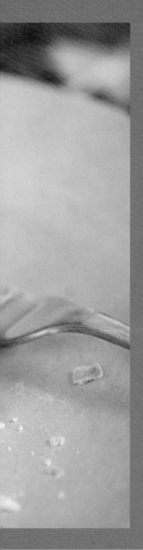

smoked trout bulbs

Serves 6 to 8

INGREDIENTS

smoked trout, about 2 ribbons per serving
cream cheese, about 2 heaped tbsp per serving
chives, finely chopped
dill, finely chopped
freshly squeezed lemon juice
freshly milled black pepper
lemon and chives for garnishing

METHOD

• Cut a square of about 20 x 20 cm cling film per person and spread the squares out onto a clean surface. Cut the ribbons of trout in half and pack a square of about 12 x 12 cm in the middle of the cling film.
• Mix the cream cheese, chives, dill, black pepper and a dash of lemon juice together. Place about 2 tablespoons in the middle of the trout squares.
• Fold the four corners of the cling film together and twist to form a ball. Refrigerate for 1 hour before serving.
• These can be prepared ahead and kept successfully in the refrigerator for 24 hours.

Trout was introduced to our rivers
and has adapted well to Cape conditions

smoorsnoek parcels

INGREDIENTS

750 g smoked snoek
2 large onions, sliced
60 ml vegetable oil
2 tbsp butter
2 cloves garlic, crushed
1 tsp dried red chillies
2 large tomatoes, peeled and diced
a generous pinch of ground cloves
freshly milled black pepper
5 medium potatoes, cubed
a handful of fresh parsley,
coarsely chopped
1 roll phyllo pastry (use as much
as required)
100 g butter, melted

METHOD

• Flake the snoek, taking care to remove all the bones. Fry the onion in the oil and butter until lightly browned. Add the garlic, chillies and tomatoes and braise for a few minutes.

• Add the flaked snoek, ground cloves and black pepper. Mix well and add the potato cubes. Simmer for 15 minutes or until the potatoes are cooked. Add the parsley and set aside to cool.

• Preheat the oven to 200°C.

• Open the phyllo pastry. Place one sheet on a working surface and cover the rest with a damp cloth to keep it from drying out.

• Cut the pastry into 4 equal squares of about 15 cm. Brush each square lightly with the melted butter making sure to cover the entire surface. Place two sheets on top of each other at an angle.

• Place 2 tablespoonfuls of smoorsnoek in the centre of the pastry and gather up the edges. Press together just above the smoorsnoek to form a parcel.

• Brush the parcel with butter and place on a sheet of parchment paper on a baking tray. Repeat until all the smoorsnoek has been used.

• Bake until golden brown.

• Serve one parcel per person as a starter.

Smoorsnoek can be frozen successfully. This is a popular dish in the Cape Malay community.

To smoor means to braise ingredients together so as to let the flavours mingle

sosaties (kebabs)

INGREDIENTS

2 Porterhouse steaks of about 250 g
each and a thickness of 2 cm
soft sundried nectarines
2 large red onions, cut into quarters
olive oil
the juice of 1 lemon
salt and freshly milled black pepper
to season

METHOD

• Soak the kebab sticks in water for a few hours to prevent them from burning on the open fire. Remove from the water and pat dry.

• Cut the steaks into cubes of about 2 x 2 cm. Toss the meat, the nectarines and the red onion quarters lightly in olive oil. Skewer the meat onto the stick, followed by the onion and then the nectarine, repeating the process once.

• Cook on a grid over an open fire. The coals must be moderate to hot. Sear the kebab on all sides before squeezing the lemon juice on top.

• Cook for about 7 to 10 minutes until brown on all sides. Remove from the heat and season with salt and pepper. Serve hot off the grill.

Marinate kebabs in a curry
marinade for a different flavour

spanspek, prawn and avocado salad

METHOD

• Heat 2 tablespoons olive oil in a pan – the pan must be very hot. Pat the prawns dry and flash fry them until they are just cooked, about 4 minutes. Squeeze the juice of half the lemon over the prawns and keep the other half. Remove from the heat and allow to cool.

• Toss the wild rocket in some olive oil and place on a platter or in a shallow bowl. Form small balls of spanspek using a 1 teaspoon measuring spoon. Place the balls on top of the rocket.

• Cut the avocado pear into slices and place on the salad. Sprinkle with a dash of freshly squeezed lemon juice.

• Cut the cucumber in half lengthways and remove the pips. Now cut the two halves into slices and scatter on top of the salad. Add the prawns and pour the cold juice from the pan over the salad.

• Sprinkle the dill and the black pepper over the salad and add some sea salt flakes just before serving – the salt enhances the sweetness of the spanspek.

INGREDIENTS

olive oil
250 g prawns, de-veined but with shells
juice of a lemon
80 g wild rocket
½ spanspek (cantaloupe), peeled and pips removed
1 avocado pear
¼ English cucumber
a handful of dill, stalks removed and coarsely chopped
freshly milled black pepper
sea salt flakes

The name was given to this melon because at the Cape the Spanish wife of Governor Sir Harry Smith preferred the melon to bacon and eggs for breakfast. One of the slaves then called it the Spanish (Spaanse) lady's bacon (spek) and later it became just spanspek.

Spanspek is our word for cantaloupe

spicy date chutney

Makes one jar of about 300 g

METHOD

• Place the dates in a bowl with the water. Allow to soak for 2 hours.

• Drain the dates and reserve 45 ml of water. Process all the ingredients using a hand blender and gradually add the water until the consistency is smooth.

• Spoon into a sterilised glass jar and keep in the refrigerator.

INGREDIENTS

200 g fresh dates, quartered and pitted
500 ml water
1 tbsp grated ginger
65 ml freshly squeezed lemon juice
65 ml freshly squeezed orange juice
1 clove garlic, peeled
¼ tsp ground cumin
¼ tsp ground allspice
1 tsp ground coriander
1 small red chilli

South Africa is one of the largest producers of medjool dates in the world

For an extra tang, ad

sweet potato and coconut milk soup

Serves 4

INGREDIENTS
2 large sweet potatoes, preferably orange-fleshed
250 ml water
400 ml coconut milk
salt and black pepper to taste
a sprinkling of ground cumin
a sprinkling of ground cinnamon
1 tbsp butter
1 medium-sized onion, thinly sliced
3 tbsp treacle sugar

METHOD
• Peel the sweet potatoes and cut them into cubes. Place in a pot and add the water.

• Cook slowly until they are soft. Drain all excess water and add the coconut milk. Season with salt and freshly milled black pepper. Add the cumin and cinnamon and allow to simmer for about 15 minutes. Remove from the heat.

• Use a stick blender to blend the soup until it has a smooth consistency. Keep it warm while you prepare the caramelised onion.

• In a pan, heat the butter and add the onion. Cook over a medium heat until they begin to brown. Add the treacle sugar and allow the mixture to caramelise and the sugar to dissolve.

• Serve the soup in bowls, topped with the caramelised onion.

touch of chilli

vegetable curry

INGREDIENTS

60 ml olive oil

1 onion, sliced

2 medium-sized aubergines, cut into large cubes

2 cloves garlic, crushed

1 tbsp curry powder, medium strength

1 can (about 400 g) chopped tomatoes in tomato juice

6 baby carrots

1 medium-sized sweet potato

400 g canned chickpeas, with the liquid

140 g mange tout

125 g baby corn

8 green patty pans

salt and pepper to taste

METHOD

• Heat the oil in a saucepan and fry the onion until transparent. Add the aubergine cubes and fry until they and the onion have browned. Remove the aubergine from the saucepan and set to one side. Turn the heat to low.

• Add the garlic, stirring continuously to ensure that the garlic doesn't turn brown as this will alter its flavour. Add the curry powder and allow the spices to heat through and release their flavours.

• Add the rest of the ingredients including the aubergines and the liquid from the chickpeas. Season and cook until the carrots are just tender, about 45 minutes.

• Serve on a bed of basmati rice or with roti.

Curry is always better the following day

vetkoek with curried mince

Makes 12 vetkoek

METHOD

• To prepare the dough, mix the dry ingredients together. Add enough lukewarm water to create a soft, bread-like dough. Cover with a cloth and leave in a warm spot to rise for about 1 hour.

• In the meantime, prepare the filling by heating the olive oil in a saucepan and frying the onion until it begins to brown. Turn the heat on low and add the curry powder. Fry for a few minutes to allow the flavours to be released. Add the minced lamb and turn the heat back up. Cook the meat making sure that it doesn't clump together by using a wooden spoon to stir and separate. As soon as the meat is cooked (about 15 minutes), turn the heat off and set aside.

• Form balls of dough about the size of a tennis ball and flatten them with your fingertips. Dust with flour and cover with a dish cloth. Allow these to rise in a warm draught-free spot for another 15 minutes.

• Heat the oil in a pot and place a few vetkoek at a time into the hot oil. Cook until puffed up and golden and then drain on a paper towel.

• To serve, cut the vetkoek open part of the way and fill with the curried minced lamb. Serve warm.

INGREDIENTS

400 g cake flour
1 tsp salt
2 tbsp sugar
1½ tsp instant dried yeast
lukewarm water, about 125 ml
canola oil, enough for deep-frying

Curried filling
30 ml olive oil
1 medium-sized onion, chopped
1 tbsp curry powder,
medium strength
500 g minced lamb

A vetkoek is a deep-fried bread ball, about the size of a tennis ball. They can be enjoyed with cheese and jam or stuffed with curried minced meat.

Baby beets are sweet in flavour

warm baby beet and crottin salad

Serves 4 to 6

METHOD

• Preheat the oven to 180°C.

• Place the beets in an oven dish and toss them in the oil to ensure they are coated. Sprinkle with the sea salt flakes. Place in the oven and bake until the beets are soft and beginning to caramelise. Remove from the oven and set to one side.

• Place the crottin in the oven for 7 to 10 minutes. Remove and carefully cut the top rind of the cheese away exposing the melted cheese. Place on a platter surrounded by the beets. Top with the micro greens and serve hot.

INGREDIENTS

12 baby beets, peeled and halved
olive oil to roast the beets in
¼ tsp sea salt flakes
1 crottin (80 g)
micro greens

nd compliment the flavour of the goat's cheese perfectly

waterblommetjie bredie

INGREDIENTS

30 ml oil to fry onions in
1 large onion, sliced
1 kg lamb neck
1 large clove garlic, crushed
1 sun-ripened tomato, peeled and chopped
500 ml water
6 small potatoes, peeled
500 g fresh or frozen waterblommetjies, cleaned
salt and pepper to taste
juice of 1 lemon

METHOD

• Heat the oil in a heavy-bottomed pot. Add the onion and cook until it goes transparent. Add the meat and brown the meat together with the onion. Add the garlic and tomato and cook, stirring all the time, until the garlic is cooked through, being careful not to let the garlic brown.

• Add the water, 100 ml at a time, and the potatoes and braise the meat on a medium to low heat for 1 hour, adding water whenever the pot has cooked dry.

• Add the waterblommetjies and season with salt and pepper. Squeeze the lemon juice into the stew and allow to simmer for another 30 minutes before serving on a bed of basmati rice.

Pond blossom stew, traditionally prepared using lamb

west coast mussel pot

Serves 4 to 6

METHOD

• Rinse the mussels under running water to get rid of bits of shell and grit. Place in a steamer and steam them in the white wine and water mixture until they open. Set aside to cool.

• To prepare the sauce, fry the leeks in the oil until they go transparent. Add the chopped dill, chervil and the crushed garlic and fry lightly. Now add the wine and then the cream and bring to the boil. Reduce the heat immediately and allow to simmer for 5 to 10 minutes to reduce a little.

• In the meanwhile, clean the mussels by removing the beard. Leave the mussels in their shells.

• Just before serving, add the mussels to the sauce and add the freshly milled black pepper. Allow the dish to heat through.

• Serve with a wedge of lemon and a hot crusty loaf.

INGREDIENTS

2 kg fresh mussels
150 ml white wine
150 ml water

Sauce
45 ml olive oil
4 to 6 leeks, finely sliced
a generous handful dill, chopped finely
a handful of chervil, chopped finely
3 large cloves garlic, crushed
250 ml good quality dry white wine
500 ml cream
freshly milled black pepper

Black mussels
are cultivated or can be picked off the rocks

Acknowledgements

The following were a valuable source of information and inspiration in the creation of this book:
Renata Coetzee, *The South African Culinary Tradition* (Cape Town, Struik, 1977)
S.J.A de Villiers, *Kook en Geniet* (Cape Town, Human & Rousseau, 1951)
Dine van Zyl, *Boerekos* (Cape Town, Human & Rousseau, 1985)
Hildagonda J. Duckitt, *Hilda's "Where is it?" of Recipes* (London, Chapman and Hall Ltd., 1891)

Special thanks to:
Clementina van der Walt, whose beautiful, locally made ceramic dishes are featured in this book
(www.clementina.co.za)
Raymond O'Grady of Hillcrest Berry Farm (www.hillcrestberries.co.za)
Rooibos Ltd. (www.rooibosltd.co.za)
Danie Pretorius, general manager, The South African Brandy Foundation (www.sabrandy.co.za)
Wines of South Africa (www.wosa.co.za)

Photography:
Neil Austen
with contributions from:
Basson van Zyl: 66, 67a
Chris Fallows: 68b, 68c, 68d, 69, 98
Hougaard Malan: Cover, 2, 14, 18, 21d, 40, 44, 45, 47, 50, 51, 54a, 67b, 73, 95
Isak Pretorius: 56c
Mount Nelson Hotel: 34
Paul Bruins: 24b, 24c, 25, 27, 29, 30a, 52, 103
Peter Brigg: 70
Peter Chadwick: 63
Richard du Toit: 81
Sophia Lindop: 61

First published by Jacana Media (Pty) Ltd in 2014
Second impression 2016

10 Orange Street
Sunnyside
Auckland Park 2092
South Africa
(+27 11) 628-3200
www.jacana.co.za

ISBN 978-1-4314-1032-3

Edited by Dominique Herman
Design and layout by Jeannie Coetzee
Set in Helvetica 8,5 pt
Job no. 002789
Printed and bound by Creda Communications

Also available as an e-book:
d-PDF ISBN 978-1-4314-1033-0

See a complete list of Jacana titles at www.jacana.co.za